Brick of Gold Publishing Company
New York City
2018

www.unlocktomorrow.com
@unlocktomorrow

www.wordsuncaged.com
@wordsuncaged

Printed in the United States of America
First Printing

ISBN 978-0-692-10612-9

Edited by Nate Fish

Brick of Gold Publishing Company
New York, NY

thebrickofgold@gmail.com
@brickofgold

FOREWORD

My name is Ray Adornetto. I'm the founder of Unlock Tomorrow. We provide programs and resources to incarcerated and formerly incarcerated young people, allowing them to share their stories and creativity.

I took a trip to Calipatria State Prison around Christmas of 2016 with my friends Scott, Jose, and Sam. Scott founded the Anti Recidivism Coalition, and is making groundbreaking progress in reforming our prisons. On that trip to Calipatria, I met a group of guys dedicated to changing their lives. I asked them to write letters to the youngsters we work with at Unlock Tomorrow. It was a straight forward request. I said, "If you could have given yourself advice twenty years ago with what you know now, what would it be?" And that's how this project all started.

About the book itself... it's a paperback because hard covers are not allowed in prisons and other correctional facilities. The title, "Man, I Wish We Would Have Known", comes from a line in the introduction written by Joel Baptiste, who also provided definitions for the glossary. It plainly states a sentiment echoed in each of the letters in the collection. We decided to use the original handwritten letters with all their imperfections as opposed to edited versions. We hope it gives you insight to who and where the guys are.

Thanks to everyone who has contributed to this book, especially the authors who spilled their hearts out in these letters. I believe when we share our stories we tap into something bigger than ourselves. That's when we can heal as individuals and as a society. I hope this book is proof of that.

Much Love,
Ray

INTRODUCTION

There is an altruistic spirit and when one becomes aware of it and its work you will then notice it all around you and it will pull you in. You will feel the need for that connection with your fellow man like you need water.

I first experienced this while serving an indeterminate *SHU term in Pelican Bay for being an extremely active and influential gang member. In the prison system, men like Scott Budnick were hard at work, and that spirit cultivated hope and humanity. These things pierced through the entire system of *CDC and *DOJ and touched me.

Fast forward a few years and I had to follow that path. I ended up in a small meeting with Scott concerning new laws and programs to educate and advance us for our eventual return to society and I got introduced to Ray Adornetto. I did not know at the time we would be friends, but that spirit I just spoke of was moving big time in his work and life. We spoke of bringing outside writers here, but soon something else took hold and we were brainstorming on ideas. In the SHU we'd say, "Man, I wish we would have known." So we started to unload our hearts on paper because we love these little homies and we do not want our little brothers and sons and families to relive our lives when hope is on the table for them.

These letters are from veterans, decades in this life and neighborhoods. If you are reading these, they are for you because even though we don't know you, we were you, and are still connected to you and we love you brothers.

Joel Baptiste

PS: Success is based on the decisions you make today for tomorrow. The past is gone and does not define you unless you fail to write your future today!

CORY SULLIVAN

35 years old
Robbery
13 years

WHATS UP YOUNG LAD,

THIS LETTER AND ITS MESSAGE IS AIMED DIRECTLY AT YOU... THERES A REASON WHY YOUR NOW READING IT, IF YOUR OPEN MINDED YOULL FIND IT.

MY NAME IS CORY AND IM 35 YEARS OLD, IM COMMITTED TO THIS CA PRISON SYSTEM FOR 13 YEARS AFTER A HOME INVASION TYPE ROBBERY I DID WHILE I WAS HIGH ON HEROIN AND SPEED. IVE ALWAYS HAD OVERWHELMING SUPER HIGH ANXIETY (JUST LIKE YOU). THE TESTOSTERONE IN YOUNG MEN COMBINED WITH TODAYS SOCIAL INFLUENCES FRUSTRATE US AND WE NEED TO CHANNEL OUR AGGRESSION. FOR ME I USED A STRONG DOSE OF MUSIC AND SKATEBOARDING WHEN I WAS REAL YOUNG TO DEAL WITH IT AND THAT WAS GOOD. THERE IS A PRECIOUS INNOCENCE WITH YOUTH, THE INNOCENCE IS ASSIGNED TO YOUTH BECAUSE IT IS A PERIOD OF GROWTH IN WHICH YOU FIND YOUR IDENTITY. ONCE YOU IDENTIFY WHAT YOU ARE AND WHO YOU ARE YOUR A MAN AND EVERYTHING YOU DO YOUR ACCOUNTABLE FOR IT. WHATS FUCKED UP IS THAT RIGHT AS WERE TRYING FIND OUT WHO WE ARE IN OUR EARLY ADOLESCENCE WERE BECOMING MATURE ENOUGH TO REALIZE THE REALITY OF THINGS AROUND US. SOME OF US SEE THAT THINGS ARE FAKE, FOUL, AND UNFAIR. WE BECOME ANGRY AND CHANNEL THE AGGRESSION WITH VIOLENCE AND WHILE TRYING TO DESTROY THE FRUSTRATIONS SOURCE, WE DESTROY OURSELVES. DRUGS, CRIME, & VIOLENCE

IM LIKE YOU IF IM GOING TO DO SOMETHING I DO IT FULL FORCE. SO WHILE I WAS SUPPOSED TO BE FINDING ME AND FIGURING OUT EVERYTHING ELSE... I WAS DOING SPEED. ADDICTION IS AN OBSESSION OF THE MIND, THE OBSESSION CRIPPLES US AND WE ACT COMPULSIVE. OUR FAMILIES START TO NOT RECOGNIZE US, WE LOSE

THE SLIPPERY GRIP WE JUST FOUND ON OURSELVES. WHEN I STARTED DOING CRIME IT WAS LITTLE BURGLARIES, TRUE TO MY EXTREME NATURE I STARTED ROBBING DRUG DEALERS AND CARRYING A GUN. I WOULD SURF AND SKATE DURING THE DAY AND FUCK AROUND ALL NIGHT. WHEN I WAS 15 I STARTED SLAMMING HEROIN ALONG WITH SMOKING THE SPEED I'D BEEN DOING, AS SOON AS I STARTED SHOOTING SPEED I LOST FULL CONTROL.

I WENT TO JUVENILLE HALL AND BECAME CLEAR HEADED ENOUGH TO START WHERE I HAD LEFT OFF IN LOOKING FOR ME, FINDING AN IDENTITY. THE GNARLIEST THING YOU CAN LATCH ONTO WHEN YOUR A DEFIANT YOUNG PUNKER SKATER, IN JUVENILLE HALL IS A SKINHEAD / GANG MENTALITY. THATS WHAT I DID. I HAD A KID WHILE I WAS IN JUVENILLE HALL. IM A PRODUCT OF MY ENVIRONMENT AND WHAT IVE BEEN THROUGH. IF YOUR ADOPTING AN IDENTITY OF A NEGATIVE NATURE, TO DEAL WITH A NEGATIVE FEELING WHILE IN A NEGATIVE PLACE, IM POSITIVE THAT IDENTITY WILL NEED TO EVENTUALLY BE RE-EVALUATED. IF THERE IS ANYTHING POSITIVE THAT COULD COME OUT OF ALL THE THINGS IVE BEEN THROUGH SINCE I DECIDED AT 16-17 TO COMMIT TO BEING A HOOLIGAN IT WOULD BE YOU LEARNING SOMETHING (EVEN SOMETHING SMALL) FROM THE EXPERIENCE... THAT WOULD REQUIRE YOU NOT BEING SO STUBBORN THAT YOU INSIST ON EXPERIENCING THE MISERY YOURSELF. EITHER COURSE CRASHES INTO THE SAME CONCLUSION. DRUGS GANGS & CRIME = MISERY AND DEATH.

DONT DEFEND YOURSELF NOW BY BEING HARDENED AS A PERSON AND THINK YOU ARE THAT PERSON. OF COURSE YOUR STRONG ENOUGH TO HANDLE ALL OF WHAT YOUR GOING THROUGH OR TO PUT IN SOME WORK. INSTEAD DEFEND YOUR FAMILY AND YOUR FUTURE SELF

BY PUTTING IN WORK ON BECOMING A DECENT MAN, BE YOUR OWN MAN,

SOON AFTER I TURNED 18 I WAS ON MY WAY TO PRISON, IN PRISON IT IS VERY DIFFICULT TO BE YOUR OWN MAN, LET ME BREAK IT DOWN FOR YOU... THERE IS MANY DIFFERENT FACTIONS GANGS AND RACES, ALL SEGREGATED. EACH RACE HAS ITS RULES WHICH ARE STRICTLY ENFORCED. EACH MAN BELONGS TO ONE OF THESE GROUPS WHETHER HE LIKES IT OR NOT. UNLESS YOUR RIGHTEOUSLY SET IN AS YOUR OWN MAN IN YOUR HEART, YOUR PEOPLE OR YOUR GANG LEADERS WILL DICTATE AND DECIDE WHO YOU ARE & WHERE YOUR GOING TO END UP AND WHEN. FUCK THAT. PRISON DOES HAVE ITS INTENSE MOMENTS... RIOTS... STABBING SOMEONE IN YOUR CELL OR ON THE YARD, ALL OF THAT IS APPLE SAUCE TO THE MISERY OF THE QUIETNESS THAT LAST FOREVER INSIDE YOUR CELL. THATS THE PART THAT YOU DONT THINK ABOUT. IF YOUR LOOKING AT OR DOING A LONG STRETCH OF TIME LEARN HOW TO LIVE IN THE CELL, BE PRODUCTIVE, EXERCIZE. AS I SPOKE ABOUT IN THE FIRST PART OF THIS LETTER WE HAVE THIS ISSUE WITH ANXIETY, WERE IMPULSIVE. UNFORTUNATELY THERES NO CURE FOR THAT, PRISON CELLS DONT HELP. FIND A CREATIVE OUTLET FOR YOUR AGGRESSION AND A TECHNIQUE FOR CALMING YOUR ANXIETY, WHEN DEALING WITH ANXIETY LET SIMPLE THINGS BE SIMPLE, DONT SPEND A BUNCH OF EFFORT & ENERGY ON THINGS YOU HAVE NO CONTROL OVER, OR ON LITTLE INSECURITIES.

NOW HOW ABOUT THE THINGS WE CAN CONTROL? IF YOUR GOING TO Y.A. OR PRISON WE CANT CONTROL THAT... WHAT YOU DO HAVE AUTHORITY OVER IS HOW YOU DO YOUR TIME. HOW YOU DECIDE RIGHT NOW TO EMBRACE WHATS IN FRONT OF YOU IS CRUCIAL IN DETERMINING THE MAN YOU WILL BECOME. TODAY START BOTHERING YOUR STAFF AND LOVED ONES ABOUT EDUCATION... ENLIGHTEN YOURSELF WITH AN OPEN

MIND TO SPIRITUALITY. YOU EDUCATE YOURSELF AND TAKE IT SERIOUSLY AUTOMATICALLY IT WILL MAKE YOU A LEADER... YOU KNOW THERES NOTHING AN O.G. CAN SAY TO A YOUNG MAN WHOSE HONORABLE, EDUCATED, SELF DRIVEN, & STRONG & POSITIVE. A LOST KID WALKING AROUND ACTING TOUGH, THERES A PLACE FOR HIM, IF YOU GOT CONCERNS OR QUESTIONS OR NEED SPECIFIC DIRECTION REACH OUT TO OUR ORGANIZATION. YOU HAVE IN FRONT OF YOU A GROWN MAN DECISION TO MAKE.

YOU ARE IN THIS PLACE THIS PLACE ISNT YOU, START BECOMING CONCERNED ONLY WITH THINGS THAT MATTER. I SUPPORT YOU AND KNOW YOUR STRUGGLE.

ALL OR NOTHING,

CORY SULLIVAN #A54456
P.O. BOX 5007
CALIPATRIA CA 92233

JESSE JAMES HOLLYWOOD

37 years old
First degree murder
Life without parole

(1)

4/20/17

Calipatria

D-4, 107 #Ac4442

Hollywood

To The Youth at Risk,

my name is Jesse James Hollywood and I've spent the last 17 years locked up in cold cells and on the run.This letter is a serious message to the youth about decisions and accountability for them.

from the time i was 14 years old i had been involved in selling mrijuana and acid...i thought it was no big deal since I wasn't involved w/hard drugs like coke,heroin,and speed.I started out selling grams and eighths,quarter ounces all the way up to sellin -g pounds and pounds of the kind weed.I had bought a house ,cars, lowriders all by the age of 18.

I was a "drug Dealer" so since I didn't want to get "Jacked I also had guns.Since i made this decision that I wanted to be "the mAN" i gave the government and any hardworking normal people the opportunity to label meaas a criminal,a thug,a drug dealer.

Sometimes life takes us this way and that withoutasking our permission and with all the wrong people I had attracted with my illicit activityI was caught in the flux of life... a haphazard juxtaposition of people and events....a murder occurred that would change mine and many others lives forever....

It was immediately all ower the news and I was deemed the "Ringleader' ....consequently i became the youngest fugitive ever on the F.B.I's most wanted list at the age of 20.(10 most wante -d0

I thought I was smart,but the long arm of the lawetracked me down in march 2005 and I was brought back to the U.S. from Brazil to face the death penalty,despite not having an extradtion treaty

In 2007 the movie "AlphadDōg"starring Justin timberlake and others based on the case came out in theaters as I awaited trial in the county jail.The movie was a precise rendition of the prosecutions theory of the case which solidified public opinion of my guilt ...

I went to trial in the summer of 2009 and was convicted of 1st degree murder ..sentenced to life without parole plus a decade.I was not present for the murderoōf my alleged victim and although the evidence at trial wasn't overwhelming,it was my decisions to be involved with dealing drugs that led to my reputation and my conviction.I allowed the government to "Label" me due to my poor decisions and that was enough.

I strongly advise the youth involved in gangs and any and all illicit activity to never give anyone this opportunity. The great president Roosevelt once said "Men aren't prisoners of fate but prisoners of their own mind.Use your mind and do not make hasty decisions.Sometimes doing nothing at all can be the best solution when a conflict arises.Simply don't react...Pray to god and give your problems to him and alot of times they will resolve themselves without any physical action on your part.

We mustn't forget that time is a master worker that heals the wounds of temporary defeat and equalizes the inequalities and rig -hts the wrongs of the world.There is nothing impossible with time!

They say that courage is the standing army of the soul which keeps it from conquest,pillage,and slavery...have the courage to make the right decisionseeven in the face of adversity.Re- -member that the kite of success rises against the wind of adversity,not with it.

the latin word cupiditas roughly translates to "Lucifers Sin"...in english cupidity means avarice greed,the strong desire for wealth or power over another..this concept is glamourized in the criminal lifestyle and respected.As human beings we need to embrace the opposite of this concept.

In latin Caritas means envisioning onesself as part of a ring of love in which each individual self has worth in itself but also as it relates to every other self.We must always think not of just ourselves but the consequences of our actions and decisions and how they will affect others.

In closing please keep in mind the latin phrase "Caritas et amor,deus ibi est"..which translates to this: Wherever caritas and love are God is...Make the right decisions and go with god.

Sincerely ,

Jesse James Hollywood #AC4442

RAY SHEPPARD

44 years old
Second degree murder
17 years to life

6/17 CALIPATRIA STATE PRISON

AT FIRST I WASN'T SURE HOW TO APPROACH THIS LETTER SINCE THIS IS A FIRST FOR ME. WHEN I WAS YOUR AGE AND IN SIMILAR SHOES I WASN'T REALLY TRYING TO HEAR SOMEONE PREACH TO ME. ESPECIALLY SOMEONE WHO NEVER WALKED THE WALK. SO HERES A LIL' ABOUT MYSELF THAT WAY YOU CAN GET A BETTER SENSE OF WHOS GETTING AT YOU.

THEY CALL ME RAY RAY AND IM ORIGINALLY FROM EAST SIDE BRUTA. IM CURRENTLY ON MY 17TH YEAR OF A 17 TO LIFE SENTENCE FOR 2ND DEGREE MURDER. BACK IN 1999 I KILLED MY LIL' HOMIE OVER A KEG OF BEER... A SENSELESS ACT. I'VE BEEN INVOLVED IN GANGS SINCE THE AGE OF 13 IN AND OUT OF THE HALLS, CAMP, GROUP HOMES, THE COUNTY, & EVENTUALLY I FOUND MYSELF HERE IN THE PEN. THIS IS MY 2ND PRISON TERM... MY 1ST WAS FOR SHOOTING TWO PEOPLE. IT WAS REDUCED TO A LESSER CRIME OF "CRIMINAL STREET GANG TERRORISM" DUE TO LACK OF EVIDENCE. FROM 1994 TO 99' I WAS IN & OUT OF PRISON MOSTLY DUE TO DRUGS. ON DEC. 4TH, 1999, I WAS AT THE WRONG PLACE AT THE WRONG TIME AND I TOOK THE LIL' HOMIES LIFE OVER NOTHING. I'VE BEEN IN THE PEN EVER SINCE BOUNCING AROUND FROM WASCO TO NEW FOLSOM... FROM NEW FOLSOM TO OLD FOLSOM... BACK TO NEW FOLSOM... TO CORCORAN... TO CENTANELLA... TO TEHACHAPI... PELICAN BAY... SALINAS VALLEY... AND FINALLY I FIND MYSELF HERE IN CALIPATRIA. SO AS YOU CAN SEE I'VE BEEN TO SOME OF THE WORST PRISONS THERE IS AND NOW I'D LIKE TO OFFER YOU SOME WORDS OF WISDOM AND ENCOURAGEMENT SO THAT YOU CAN AVOID SOME OF THE SAME MISTAKES I'VE MADE.

THE BIGGEST ADVICE I CAN OFFER YOU, BECAUSE IT WAS THE ROOT OF ALL MY TROUBLES... IS TO FIND A WAY TO STAY OFF OF DRUGS PERIOD. 90% OF ALL MY PROBLEMS, BOTH HERE IN THE PEN & ON THE STREETS, WERE DUE TO DRUGS IN SOME SHAPE OR FORM. HERES SOMETHING TO THINK ABOUT. OVER 90% OF THE PRISON POPULATION ARE IN HERE OVER DRUGS.

OVER 90% OF THE STABBINGS IN HERE ARE DUE TO DRUGS. WE TEND TO DO THINGS WE WOULD NEVER DO IF WE WERE CLEAN. WHEN WERE ON DRUGS OUR MINDS ARE CLOUDED, WE CANT THINK CLEARLY AND THEREFORE WE MAKE MISTAKES IN LIFE. SOMETIMES THESE MISTAKES ARE DEADLY & COST US DEARLY. SO IF YOU COULD FIND A WAY TO STAY OFF AND AWAY FROM DRUGS YOUR ALREADY WINNING. YOUR ALREADY AHEAD OF THE GAME. YOUR CHANCES OF SUCCESS ARE THAT MUCH GREATER. GUESS WHAT?.. I WAS HIGH WHEN I TOOK THE LIL' HOMIES LIFE. IF ONLY I KNEW WHAT IM SHARING WITH YOU NOW... MAYBE THINGS WOULDVE TURNED OUT DIFFERNTLY.

THE LAST THING I WOULD LIKE TO SHARE WITH YOU IS LEARN TO BE YOUR OWN MAN... YOUR OWN PERSON, CONTROL YOUR OWN DESTINY. STAY OUT OF THAT GANG MENTALITY AND WAY OF LIFE. THE MINUTE YOU START GANG BANGING YOU BECOME A FOLLOWER. YOU STOP THINKING FOR YOURSELF AND SET YOURSELF UP FOR FAILURE. I'VE BEEN GANG BANGING OUT THERE IN THE HOOD AND IN HERE AS A SUREÑO SINCE I WAS 13. IM 44 YEARS OLD NOW AND AS OF LAST YEAR I DENOUNCED MY HOOD... BEING A SUREÑO... AND ANYTHING & EVERYTHING REMOTELY RELATED TO GANG POLITICS. I DECIDED IT WAS TIME TO HANG THEM UP AND TIME TO REGAIN CONTROL OF MY LIFE & DESTINY. AFTER ALL THESE YEARS OF BANGING, HURTING PEOPLE, USING DOPE, IN & OUT THE SYSTEM I FINALLY WOKE UP ONE DAY AND REALIZED LIFE IS TO SHORT FOR THIS NONSENSE. AFTER ALL THAT WAS SAID AND DONE I HAVE NOTHING TO SHOW FOR IT AND TO TOP IT OFF IM STILL STUCK IN HERE.

I CAN GO ON AND ON WITH THIS LETTER BUT I DONT WANT TO BORE YOU. SO I'LL END IT WITH THIS... THE WORLD IS A BIG BEAUTIFUL PLACE FULL OF OPORTUNITIES. FIND WHAT IT IS YOUR GOOD AT AND TURN IT INTO SUCCESS. THERES A BETTER WAY OF LIFE. WE WERN'T MEANT TO BE LOCKED UP. GOD BLESS YOU & YOURS AND GOOD LUCK.

SINCERELY...
EX-GANGMEMBER - RAYRAY SHEPPARD

ABEL ARANDA

35 years old
Assault with a deadly weapon
20 years

ABEL ARANDA
*K47141

MAY, 2017

THIS LETTER IS DEDICATED TO ALL OF YOU THAT HAVE NOT YET BEEN EXPOSED TO THE LIFESTYLE THAT'S BEYOND YOUR WALLS AND THAT ARE CURRENTLY OR HAVE BEEN MY PRISON WALLS FOR THE LAST 20 YEARS. IF THERES ANYTHING I CAN SHARE WITH YOU, ITS THAT I WAS JUST LIKE SOME OF YOU, HURTING, ANGRY, AND NOT TRULY KNOWING HOW TO DEAL OR COPE WITH LIFE AT A YOUNG AGE.

I CAME FROM A BROKEN HOME WHERE I FELT THAT I DIDN'T BELONG. MY RELATIONSHIP WITH MY MOM AND 2 SISTERS WAS VERY STRAIND. BUT ITS THE RELATIONSHIP THAT I HAD WITH MY DAD THAT REALLY FUCKED ME UP. HE WAS PHYSICALLY, MENTALLY, EMOTIONALLY, AND VERBALLY ABUSIVE TOWARDS ALL OF US. BUT MY MOM AND I REALLY GOT IT THE WORST. MY DAD SUFFERS FROM MENTAL ISSUES, AT ONE POINT WAS AN ALCOHOLIC, AND WAS (AND STILL IS) A VERY ANGRY PERSON. WE WERE ALL SCARED OF HIM. HE WAS JUST THAT TYPE OF PERSON. BUT THAT FEAR FOR ME, SLOWLY STARTED TO COMBINE WITH RESENTMENT. AND THAN CAME THE ANGER AND HATE. I HAD A SPECIAL KIND OF HATE FOR MY DAD. KIND OF LIKE HE HAD FOR HIS OWN FATHER AT ONE POINT. GROWING UP MY DAD HAD IT PRETTY ROUGH TOO. BUT NOT REALIZEING OR TRULY UNDERSTANDING, HE WAS REPEATING THAT SAME CYCLE WITH ME. WITHOUT REALIZEING IT, I BECAME A LOT LIKE MY DAD. HIS ANGER BECAME MY OWN.

I STARTED ACTING OUT. AND EVEN THOUGH MY PARENTS PROVIDED FOR US, I STARTED STEALING.

IN ELEMENTRY SCHOOL I STAYED IN THE PRINCIPALS OFFICE. IF IT WASN'T ONE THING IT WAS ANOTHER. FIGHTING WAS MY SPECIALTY. ESPECIALLY AS I GOT OLDER. I ENDED UP GETTING KICKED OUT OF EVERY JR. HIGH SCHOOL I WENT TO. INTILL FINALLY THE SCHOOL DISTRICT GOT TIRED OF MY SHIT AND EXPELLED ME FROM THE WHOLE DISTRICT. BY THEN I WAS 14 YEARS OLD, HAD ALREADY JOINED A GANG, STARTED HAVING UNPROTECTED SEX AND SMOKEING WEED.

THAT SUMMER IS WHEN THINGS REALLY STARTED TAKEING A DRASTIC TURN. MY PARENTS SPLIT UP, MY RELATIONSHIP WITH MY MOM AND 2 SISTERS GOT EXTREMLY WORSE. WITH MY HOMEBOYS I FOUND THE ACCEPTANCE I WAS LOOKING FOR. WITH THEM I HAD THAT SENSE OF FAMILY I DIDN'T HAVE WITH MY OWN FAMILY. I FINALLY FELT THAT I BELONGED. FROM THERE ON IT WAS ALL ABOUT GANG BANGING, GUNS, AND GIRLS. AND THEN I STARTED FUCKING WITH METH. I WENT FROM STEALING LITTLE KNICK KNACK THINGS TO STEALING CARS. I DIDN'T CARE THAT THEY BELONGED TO SOMEONE OR THAT IT WAS A ONLY MEANS OF TRANSPORTATION FOR THEIR OWNERS. AS ASHAME AS I AM TO SAY IT, I STOLE FROM MY OWN FAMILY. IN MY SELFCENTERED AND SELFISH ADDICTION TO GANG BANGING AND DRUGS, I LOST ALL CONSIDERATION AND REGARD FOR ALL THOSE OUTSIDE MY NEW FAMILY, MY GANG.

ON JULY, 16, 1995, I AND 2 OF MY HOMEBOYS COMMITTED AN ATTEMPT ON THE LIFE OF ALBERT TEMORRES. A 15 YEAR OLD RIVAL GANG-MEMBER. A HUMAN BEING. ON AUGUST, 18, 1995. MY DAD TOOK ME TO THE POLICE STATION. I WAS ARRESTED AND BOOKED INTO AN ORANGE COUNTY JUVENILE HALL. IN COURT WE WERE FOUND UNFIT TO BE TRIED AS JUVENILES AND WERE BOUND OVER TO SUPERIOR COURT SO THAT WE COULD BE TRIED AS ADULTS. WE WERE LOOKING AT 45 YEARS TO LIFE. BUT IN THE END WE TOOK AN ASSULT WITH A DEADLY WEAPON CHARGE. A DEAL OF 20 YEARS WITH 85%.

AND SO BEGAN MY 22 YEARS OF INCARCERATION. FROM JUVI I WENT TO A FEW OTHER HOUSING FACILITIES WITHIN THE COUNTY. AFTER SENTENCING I MADE MY WAY THROUGH Y.A. I WAS SUPPOSE TO BE HOUSED THERE TILL I TURNED 18. BUT I ENDED UP GETTING KICKED OUT FOR FIGHTING. I BECAME A Y.A REJECT. AT 16 ALMOST 17 YEARS OF AGE, I FOUND MYSELF BEING TRANSFERED TO AN ADULT PRISON. ALMOST 2 YEARS INTO MY INCARCERATION AND I WAS ENTERING A WHOLE NEW WORLD OF EXTREME VIOLENCE, MURDER, MANIPULATION, AND DRUG ABUSE. I CAN'T SAY I WASN'T A LITTLE SCARED. BUT I SOON LEARNED THAT IF I WANTED TO SURVIVE, I HAD TO HARDEN MY MIND AND HEART. AFTER I LEFT RECEPTION, I FOUND MYSELF ON THE BUS HEADED TO HIGH DESERT STATE PRISON.

AT THAT TIME H.D.S.P WAS CONSIDERED ONE OF THE WORST AND MOST VIOLENT PRISONS AROUND. I SOON STARTED TO ADAPT TO MY NEW ENVIRONMENT AND TOOK ON MY NEW ROLE AS A SUREÑO GANGMEMBER.

AS SUREÑOS WE BECAME ONE AND MOVED AS ONE. ALL THAT GANGBANGING WE DID ON THE STREETS DIDN'T MEAN SHIT IN HERE. IN HERE OUR WORST ENEMIES ON THE STREETS COULD EASILY BECOME OUR NEW BEST FRIENDS. WE WERE SUPPOSE TO HAVE EACHOTHERS BACKS. IT WAS A COOL CONCEPT. ESPECIALLY FOR SOMEONE LIKE MYSELF AND SO MANY OTHERS WHO WERE SEEKING ACCEPTANCE. AND SO IT REMAINED THAT WAY BUT ONLY FOR A LITTLE WHILE. I SOON STARTED TO SEE A LOT OF BULLSHIT BEHIND DRUGS AND POLITICS. A LOT OF GREED AND MANIPULATION.

AND THEN ON SEPTEMBER, 27, 1998 8 MONTHS INTO MY STAY IN WHAT WAS SUPPOSE TO BE MY NEW HOME, I STABBED AND KILLED RUDOLPH RIVERA A FELLOW SUREÑO. A HUMAN BEING. THIS IS WHERE I REALLY NEED YOU GUYS TO UNDERSTAND THAT BACK THEN AND EVEN NOW, YOU HAVE TO WALK A FINE LINE IN ANYTHING AND EVERYTHING YOU DO. IF YOU STRAY FROM THAT LINE, YOU'RE GOING TO GET CHECKED. AND THAT MEANS YOU'RE MOST LIKELY GOING TO GET STABBED OR YOU'RE GOING TO HAVE TO STABB SOMEONE ELSE. THATS JUST THE WAY IT WAS AND STILL IS.

I SOON FOUND MYSELF IN THE HOLE FACING MURDER CHARGES. I WAS HOUSED BY MYSELF AND COULD ONLY GO TO YARD BY MYSELF. I WAS TOLD THAT BECAUSE I WAS STILL A 17 YEAR OLD MINOR, THAT'S HOW IT HAD TO BE. WHEN I FINALLY TURNED 18, I WAS ABLE TO GO TO YARD WITH THE REST OF THE SUREÑOS. AND SO TIME WENT ON, AND THEN ONE DAY I WAS WORKING OUT WHEN 4 SUREÑOS JUMPED ON ME. THEY CUT AND STABBED ME. NOTHING SERIOUS. BUT ALL THAT DID WAS ADD FUEL TO MY FIRE. I WAS PLACED BACK ON SINGLE CELL STATUS AND COULD NO LONGER GO TO YARD WITH THE REST OF THE SUREÑOS. I WANTED TO GO BACK OUT THERE AND SO I ASKED TO GO BACK OUT THERE BUT I WAS DENIED. I WANTED REVENGE AND I KNEW WHO I WANTED TO GET. IN MY MIND, I HAD JUST MURDERED SOMEONE. I KNEW WHAT I WAS CAPABLE OF AND SO DID EVERYONE ELSE. I HAD THIS FALSE SENSE OF PRIDE AND A NEW IMAGE TO LIVE UP TO. IF ANYONE GOT IN THE WAY OF THAT, I WAS WILLING TO PROVE MYSELF BY ANY MEANS NECESSARY.

AND SO WENT ON MY WAY OF THINKING INTILL ONE DAY I MET JOSE VERA (SAD BOY) A FELLOW SUREÑO WITH TIES TO THE MEXICAN MAFIA. WE STARTED TALKING AND SOON BECAME FRIENDS. HE STARTED ADVISING ME ON EVERYTHING THAT HAD HAPPEND. HE MADE ME REALIZE

THAT NONE OF WHAT I WAS GOING THROUGH, WAS WORTH IT. HE ASKED ME TO THINK ABOUT MY MOM AND WHAT SHE WAS GOING THROUGH. I HAD NEVER LOOKED AT IT FROM THAT POINT OF VIEW. EVERYTHING THAT HAD HAPPEND UP INTILL THAT POINT, WAS ALL ABOUT ME. I NEVER STOPPED TO THINK ABOUT WHAT I HAD AND WAS PUTTING HER THROUGH. WITH TIME AND REFLECTING, I MADE WHAT AT THE TIME SEEMED LIKE ONE OF THE HARDEST DECISIONS I WOULD EVER HAVE TO MAKE. I DECIDED TO STEP AWAY FROM THE GANG LIFESTYLE. BUT THAT BECAME A PROCESS IN ITSELF. I WAS STILL FACING MURDER CHARGES AND I SOON STARTED GOING TO COURT. I WAS NOW FACING LIFE IN PRISON.

I HAD NEVER BEEN ONE TO GIVE A FUCK ABOUT CONSEQUENCES, BUT NOT HAVING LIFE TO HAVING LIFE WAS A BIG REALITY CHECK. I WAS PRETTY SCARED AT THAT POINT. I DIDN'T WANT TO SPEND THE REST OF MY LIFE IN HERE. THE D.A ENDED UP OFFERING ME A VOLUNTARY MANSLAUGHTER DEAL, 11 YEARS WITH 85%. I TOOK IT. THE 20 YEARS I CAME IN WITH BECAME A 31 YEAR SENTENCE. A FEW MONTHS AFTER SENTENCING I FOUND MYSELF ON MY WAY TO THE CORCORAN S.H.U (SECURITY HOUSING UNIT). I WAS 18 ALMOST 19 AND WAS NOW BEING HOUSED AROUND THE WORST OF THE WORST. IN THE SHU ITS A WHOLE —

DIFFRENT WORLD. YOU'RE SECLUDED FOR 21 OUT OF 24 HOURS A DAY. MY STAY THERE WAS SHORT. I ENDED UP GETTING TRANSFERED TO THE PELICAN BAY SHU. IT WAS DEFINITLY AN EXPERIENCE I'LL NEVER FORGET. A LITTLE OVER 3 YEARS AND A HALF OF HOLE AND SHU TIME. AND I WAS FINALLY ON MY WAY OUT. BUT I STILL HAD TO GO THROUGH THE PROCESS OF BECOMING AN EX-GANGMEMBER.

ONCE I WAS FINALLY CLEARED, I WAS PLACED ON A P.C (PROTECTIVE CUSTODY) YARD OVER AT NEW FOLSOM STATE PRISON. HERE THERE WAS EX-SUREÑOS, EX-NORTEÑOS, EX-SKINHEADS, EX-CRIPS AND BLOOD GANG-MEMBERS. AS WELL AS MEXICAN MAFIA, NUESTRA FAMILY, ARYAN BROTHERHOOD, AND BLACK GORILLA FAMILY DROP-OUTS. I COULD TELL RIGHT AWAY THINGS FROM HERE ON OUT WOULD BE DIFFRENT. AND IT WAS. BUT I STILL HAD A CHIP ON MY SHOULDER. EVERYTHING THAT I HAD GONE THROUGH UP INTILL THAT POINT HAD REALLY FUCKED ME UP. I STARTED DRINKING AND SMOKING WEED AGAIN. AS I WENT FROM ONE PRISON TO ANOTHER, I CONTINUED USING AND GETTING INTO TROUBLE. METH, HEROIN, PILLS, AND THE NEEDLE BECAME MY ESCAPE AS THE YEARS STARTED PILEING ON. I WAS STILL ANGRY; VIOLENT, AND HAD A NEW PROFOUND HATE FOR LIFE.

I WAS MISERABLE! I STARTED DROWNING IN MY OWN SELF PITY. THE FACT THAT I WAS ONLY 14 WHEN I GOT BUSTED AND EVERYTHING ELSE

THAT HAD HAPPEND, STARTED WEIGHING ON ME. I STARTED BLAMEING GOD WITHOUT REALLY LOOKING AT MYSELF. I WAS IN REALLY BAD SHAPE AND WOULD REMAIN THAT WAY FOR A VERY LONG TIME. BUT THEN AROUND MY 17TH YEAR I STARTED HEARING ABOUT SCOTT BUDNICK AND WHAT BECAME KNOWN AS (SB260). IT WAS IN ITS EARLY STAGES. BUT I COULD FEEL THAT LITTLE GLIMMER OF HOPE. WHEN (SB260) FINALLY PASSED, SHIT GOT REAL, REALLY FAST!

I NOW HAD AN OPPORTUNITY TO GO HOME SOONER. BUT I NOW HAD TO PREPARE FOR A BOARD HEARING: KEEP IN MIND, I'M NOT A LIFER SO A BOARD HEARING WAS NEVER IN MY FUTURE. I REMEMBER IN THE PAST HEARING LIFERS TALK ABOUT BOARD AND HOW THEY WERE PREPARING. BUT I COULD CARELESS AT THAT TIME. I WAS ACTUALLY THANKFUL I DIDN'T HAVE TO GO THROUGH THAT PROCESS. WELL THAT CHANGED. AND I DIDN'T HAVE A DAMN THING TO SHOW THE BOARD MEMBERS. IT WAS A VERY STRESSFUL SITUATION AND I DIDN'T HANDLE IT VERY WELL. BUT I SOON FOUND MY SELF INVOLVED IN SELF-HELP PROGRAMS. AND IT WAS THERE THAT I FOUND THE HELP I NEEDED TO UNDERSTAND MY ANGER, MY POTENTIAL FOR VIOLENCE, AND MY DRUG ABUSE.

WITH AN OPENMIND AND THE WILLINGNESS, I STARTED DEALING WITH THESE ISSUES. I KNEW I COULDN'T DO IT ON MY OWN. BUT I DIDN'T

HAVE TO. I HAD HELP EVERY STEP OF THE WAY. THOSE LIFERS THAT I SPOKE OF BEFORE BECAME A GUIDE TO MY REHABILITATION. THEY SET THE EXAMPLE, I JUST FOLLOWED. MY FAMILY ALSO PLAYED A VERY IMPORTANT ROLE IN EVERYTHING POSITIVE I'M DOING. IF IT WASN'T FOR THEM I WOULD'VE GAVE UP ON LIFE YEARS AGO. THEY'VE BEEN HERE FOR ME SINCE DAY ONE ESPECIALLY MOM'S. AND SO WHEN I COULDN'T DO SHIT FOR MYSELF, I DID IT FOR THEM. I OWE THEM MORE THAN THEY'LL EVER KNOW.

I'VE NOW COME TO TERMS WITH WHAT ARE LIFES TERMS FOR ME. I ACCEPT AND TAKE RESPONSIBILITY FOR MY DECISIONS, ACTIONS, AND CHOICES. THERES NOBODY TO BLAME. NOT EVEN GOD. I DON'T BELIEVE HE CHOSE ANY OF THIS FOR ME. HE GAVE ME FREEWILL. AND EVEN THOUGH MY LIFE WAS IMPACTED BY AN ANGRY AND VIOLENT FATHER, WITH MY FREEWILL, I CHOSE TO JOIN A GANG, DO DRUGS, AND COMMITT CRIMES. I NOW CHOOSE TO DO THE RIGHT THINGS THAT WILL ALLOW ME TO CONTINUE MOVING IN A POSITIVE DIRECTION.

I'M 36 YEARS OLD NOW. AND I DON'T WANT WHAT HAPPEND TO ME TO HAPPEN TO ANY OF YOU. I'M A PRIME EXAMPLE OF WHAT YOU SHOULDN'T END UP LIKE. DON'T LET 22 YEARS OF MY LIFE, BECOME YOURS. BECAUSE AS YOU CAN SEE THROUGH MY STORY, ITS NOT WORTH IT. I KNOW LIFE SOMETIMES ISN'T FAIR AND IT MAY SEEM LIKE THE ODDS -

ARE AGAINST US, BUT ITS WHAT WE DO WITH THOSE ODDS THAT DEFINE NOT ONLY WHOM WE BECOME, BUT WHERE WE END UP IN LIFE. SO PLEASE GET HELP IF ITS OFFERED, EDUCATE YOUR SELF, AND MOST IMPORTANTLY, BE WHO YOU WANT TO BE AND NOT WHO YOU THINK YOU SHOULD BE. I WISH EVERY SINGLE ONE OF YOU A GOOD LIFE AND SUCCESS IN EVERYTHING YOU PUT YOUR MIND TO.

SINCERELY, ABEL ARANDA JR.
#K412191

JEREMIAH LONG

31 years old
Voluntary manslaughter
25 years

" Hoping for the Best "

There is a doorway that compromises the essence of exposure where the gift of stability shelters us from the storm of screams. The advice cost nothing but the discipline to execpt it. We must not be blinded by the mist nor guess the method of it's perpose, to find a place where damage is not a religion of hurt,but a solution in the motion laeding to a peacful way of life.

" To change my ways '"

As my soul breaks like clouds on the horizon I find myself traped locked down behind these walls. My mind is down the drain with so much pain I'm comming apart and acting strange. I guess this is what happens when your locked in a cage. Nothing will change till you turn the page so I find syself reading, sitting center stage, because this is my life and I'll live it my way. Take it breath by breath,day by day,I will have to work hard to change my ways.

"Last Stop"

As we sit and listen to the silence we play games to keep the dark away.While other people sleep we stay up both ends of the night.Lurking like a wolf in the shadows I will not find myself in a wild and loney place.I will not die in the dark where echos live,because we will stand tall in the eye of the storm and hold hands as we take a walk through the fire.We will vanish and become part of the bone garden, It's a freefall lullaby with the monkey in a raincoat. The last stop on the sunset express.

"Learn and Overcome"

We are capeable of more than we think we can do. Because if you don't know the human spirit is enormously difficult to destroy. We are bound together by morals and strong virtues.Pain, change , and growth are all conected as we move forward.We are forced to reach inside to find what we really believe and are capable of.I want to remind you there's no shortcuts to any place worth going. So you must learn the importants of being your own champion . Strive to make a differance and don't ever give up,because we all have stumbling blocks the important thing is to turn them into stepping stones.

Poems by Jeremiah Long

From Santa Cruz housed at Calipatria State Prison D-Yard

MARCELO IRIART

53 years old
First degree murder
25 years

5.16.2017

My name is Marcelo, born and raised in Los Angeles Ca. I was rased by a sigal parent of one (mother), who rased 5 kids on her own. She was a hard working parent as a nurse at a hospitol for many years. Mom's had an addiction which was alcohol. Most of my childhood growing up I felt abanded and rejected as a kid, because all my family had issues with drinking and held resentments towards each other for many unknown reasons. I develope my own defects of character at a young age which was also alcohol, anger, low self esteem, Insecurity, self Centerness, lying, dishonesty, greed, and fear.

At the age of 9 yrs old, I was influenced by other older kids to steal money to buy glue and beer. This was my first experience with sniffing glue and drinking beer. This changed my attitude and character towards my mom, family members, friends, school, and people. I resented my mom and all values in our home. I got in trouble at school at a young age, was hanging around with the wrong people who drank, smoked weed, sniffed pant, ditched school, stole cars, broke into homes, and broke the law. I was in and out of placements, juvenile halls, camps, and got in trouble with the law all my teenage years. I became an alcoholic, used pcp very heavily, broke into houses to support my addiction. I joined a gang in E.L.A. at the age of 13teen. because I wanted to be accepted, respected, appreciated, and in control. My out of control behavior and addiction only got me deeper into trouble. At the age of 17teen I committed a serious crime 1st degree murder robbery, and I murdered an innocent man by the name Paul Paez age 50, and got $20.00 off him just to meet my needs because I had an addiction and I wanted to impress my homeboys I was down.

In April of 1981, I was arrested for murder/robbery, and I was 17teen, went to court and in 1982 I was sentance to 25 yrs, to life in prison. At 18teen I was sent to San Quentin Prison, and while we were being processed I witnessed my first violence as another inmate stabbed another inmate and took his life within seconds. In fear I surrounded myself with

with other peers from the E.L.A. area, so I could be sucured by their presence. I then joined a prison gang known as the Surenős. I committed violent crimes on inmates and staff. I wanted to be accepted, respected, and show my loyalty to the surenős I was down for the cause, besides it was all about survival showing no fear.

After 22 yrs of violence, drugs, and alcohol abuse on the mainline and proving my loyalty to the sureno gang, I didn't have the heart for representing the prison gang. I seen enough stabbings, deaths, and young men die before my eyes, and at the age of 40 years old I couldn't live this lifestyle as a gang member all my life. I hated my life and who I was, and I wanted to change it all around for me and my family, who loved me and always stood by my side.

In 2003, I left the lifestyle as a gang member and seeked a new journey in my life to find my identity as to who I truly was, and seek some peace. Once I started removing these mask and false character of different false beliefs I betraded myself to be, I started developing self confidence within my self I could change and become someone productive in life for myself, family, friends, community, and society. I wrote down my goals I wanted to achieve in my life which was an education, job skills, and self-help programs. I accomplished my High School Dipolma, Completed two trades Electrical/Welding, joined AA-NA and became a chairman, and been drug and alcohol free for 10 yrs. I pratidipate in Criminal Gangmembers Anonymous, Gang Awareness, Alternative to Violence Project, Walk the Yard Mentor, Straight Life Youth Diversion, Bible study (TUMI) The Urban Ministry Institute, I'm an Overseer of Grace Chapel Prison, and I have accomplished many other goals in my life. I have been blessed with a beautiful woman and we've been together for 7yrs. and we plan on getting married once I'm free! But the self-help programs have taugh me great insight on how to apply these principles to my daily life and deal with my character defects and false beliefs that brought me to make poor choices in life. Now after looking back at my life in a mirror as who I was back then, and who I have become now, I'm not ashamed to love and forgive myself. I'm happy and at peace within myself, I don't hold no regrates towards anyone nor do I blame anyone for my wrong choices in life, but take responsibility for my own actions in life.

#3

My main goal now is to share my life story and testimony with other young youths who may be falling into a false belief that joining a gang is a lifestyle of being Cool and accepted. But I'm here to tell you that joining a gang will destroy your life and either kill you or land you in prison for life. My Criminal activities on the streets and in prison Kept me lock up for 37 yrs. and away from my loved ones. I lost all my family members behind Cancer, grandmother, sister, brother, and my mom last year. Don't throw your life away behind a false belief that has no value. The only true people who care is family who will never abandon you, but will be there until the end. Family, you must hold on too, because they will take care of you with your needs, money, packages, writing paper and stamps, Collect Calls, visits on Sat - Sun - Holidays - but homeboys wont, they'll abandon you never carring about your needs.

I traveled this road with false beliefs and hope, that I would never get out of prison or see family again, but die in prison by either violence, drugs, physical heath issues or old age. Well I'm here to tell you, I survived these ruff years in prison and on Dec 8, 2016, I finally received a parole date after serving 37 yrs. on a 25 yrs. to Life in prison. I'm now 53 yrs. old and I'm serving a Two year sentance for a possion of a weapon while in prison from 1987, but the best part is I'm no longer a lifer in prison but have a parole date 4.8.2018, and I'm free!

I hope I can give some inspiration to some young youth not to head down this same path I once walked and lived. If I Can make the write choices and turn it around, so can you. Just surround yourself with some positive influence like Self-help programs and with people who care about You, and believe me, their are people who care. If you are serious about Change and you want help We can help you. Are door and hearts are open for you. "It's never to late to walk away and Cry out for help, we here to guide you and be your rock."

Respectfully
Marcelo Iriart
C 45539 Calipatria
State Prison

MARCO PEREZ

35 years old
First degree murder
50 years to life

Marco Perez #AB5737
Calipatria State Prison
D-4 #136

Choosing Time And Words Carefully

4-30-17

They say that these two are ireplaceable. I know this to be true. For many years I didn't give a damn about a thing. In the streets, the halls, y.a., and in prison.

Living in the streets and in here all we care about is our 'hood, status, drugs, and coming out on top during any situation. Growing up we are taught the gang codes, rules, beliefs, habits, and manners. When anyone challanges these values we do what we have to, to protect our honor and loyalty. Living and dying for the cause.

Starting off I want to let you know that im just like you. I started messing up at twelve years old, getting introduced to crime and drugs. At thirteen I got jumped into the hood and lived for it. I loved my 'hood, my homies, my reputation, and doing everything for it. So much that my time revolved around it causing me to catch a 50 to Life sentence.

This world we live in is chaotic but by no means does it justify our lifestyles. We are not a product of our enviroment! We are a product of our choices! Suprisingly it took me 12 years to realize that I was living a lie. A life that was of total contradiction.

Now allow me to give you my point of view having lived both sides of life. How can we love our family when we show different. We cause them so much pain, sadness, dissapointment, anger, and many problems. We do care about them but, we rather spend our time running the streets and working for our gang. This is living life in self-destruction.

Marco Perez #AB5737

Our thinking and behavior became twisted. In reality we don't even like ourselves. How can we put ourselves in danger, isolation, bitterness, wrecks, and dangerous habits causing madness in our lives.

Life in general is a struggle. On the inside or out. We have to watch our words, For they become our actions, Each action having it's effect. We have the power of choice. It is up to each of us individually to decide. I'm not here to make you do anything, because no one has that type of power. I'm just here to guarantee you, that theres more to life than living in self-destruction, pure insanity.

For many years I struggled with many things pride, acceptance, conflicts and many other issues. What helped me to see life differently was education, books, and observation of everything. No one can take this from you. In fact you will gain knowledge that will help you in countless situations. No one wants to be taken advantage of or manipulated. I sure as hell dont want to be told what to do by another man and I'm sure neither do you. Dont get me wrong I didnt do anything by myself. Many older homies helped me but it was these who knew better. Give yourself the chance to spend your time wisely.

Another thing that helped me to be my own man is my own opinion. I use to allow others opinion become my own opinion causing me to act recklessly. This just means that we shouldn't allow other people to have the effect of messing up our life, them becoming our dictators. Just be who you are

Marco Perez # AB5737

and say what you mean, because in the end those who matter dont mind, and those who mind dont matter. Real stuff.

I know many of you are facing harsh times. I was tried as an adult while I was a juvenile as well. Although this may be the case, dont give up or give in. Maintain strong and seek to improve your life. Many things are changing in the system. Continue to be open-minded because there are many opportunities. I encourage you to take action in choosing your time and words carefully, because they are irreplaceable. There is hope.

Respectfully,
Marco Perez
Marco Perez

EDGAR GARCIA

29 years old
Murder
26 years to life

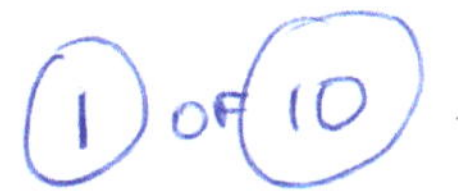

"This is my story, Don't let it be Yours" By. Edgar Garcia #AI1860

Hello to whomever is reading this letter. I hope and I pray that while your reading this letter you can take some time to sit and reflect hard on the lifestyle you decide to take from now on. I want you to Know that Im not reaching out to you, to in any way preach down to you, lecture you, or even judge you for anything that you have done. But I ask that you hear me out, cause maybe as you read my real life testimony, you'll be able to maybe pin-point and see some familiar signs that I myself missed as a kid. Maybe you'll even relate with what I went through, who Knows?

My name is Edgar Garcia, currently an inmate in a California State Prison. Im serving a twenty-six year to-life sentence, for the murder of someone who was just like us, a human being.

I grew up with two loving parent's, a handfull of sisters, and one brother. My life was a.... pretty normal one, I had the occasional fights with my brother, arguements with my sister's ect. But at the end of the day we still were a family. — My parent's gave us all they could. Provided each one of us with clothes on our backs, shoe's on our feet, and a roof to live under. My life wasn't that bad. And I Know your probably wondering why I went so wrong then huh...? Let me honestly tell you, that im still figuring all that out today. —

Now though I can successfully pin-point a lot of internal as well as external factors that played a major role in my early life. And I deal with those factors now, and I pray that it won't be late for you to approach those factors in your life. To deal with the process of reflecting and catching those signs on time. Because I can honestly say to you that its a lot better and wiser to deal with your issues now, while you still can and are at odds with the help and support of many.

When I was about eleven year's old, I dealt with something I wasn't aware of. Low Self-esteem. I had Low self-esteem because at eleven my parents and I moved out of my hometown.

I was force to leave behind my best friend's, my sports team, and even the girls I was starting to develope a crush for. I didn't like it, but it was something I had no control over because I was only a Kid.

I remember that because of us moving away from my hometown I started dealing with a lot of insecurities, insecurities I wasn't aware of. In one place I had what seemed like a hundreth friend's, and in this other place I had nothing. I had to start over, meet new people, new friend's, and I wasn't up nor had the energy to deal with all that. I wanted my old life back, but that life was history and a part of my distant memories.

In school, I was always good. In fact I loved goin to school, I wasn't a geek or nerd, or at least not that I thought I was. But I liked school, I gave it my all, I was motivated. I had teacher's that were the best to me, always willing to help me and making me feel comfortable. Maybe you relate to this, if you ever had a teacher or someone that was willin to help you with school. — And lets not forget about "friends". Because I had ton's of them. And for some reason the friend's I had always looked up to me, no matter were I went. It was always that way. My friends loved me, and I loved them back.

Man we would do everything together. Go everywhere with eachother, and when we weren't in the streets or even at the park. We were at someones house playing video games or watching movies. We were all unseparateable. Like gum stuck to a shoe, the more you tried rubbing it out, the more it stuck.

When we moved away I had none of this. Most of it because I wasn't willing to start over. So I would avoid goin to school, and make up excuses to my parents' of me feeling sick, that way I would just stay at home. In all reality I was only isolating myself from the world. And I wasn't allowing myself the opportunity to meet new people. And whenever I would go to school, I was labeled as being the "new kid". — I became a little anti-social, and at lunch I would find myself eating alone. And it would feel as though I was a freak show or something, with all eyes on me. So my insecurities would kick in, and I would walk over to the nurces office, ask to go home because I wasn't feeling well. And this behavior was repeated for like the first two weeks of school. I was running away from my problems, something I had never done before:. — But when I did decide to stay at school for all six periods of the day. It all felt easy. — I had survived. And I told myself that if I had done it once already, I could sure as hell do it againg. And I did.

Something amazing happend when I did stay at school, for all six periods of the day. I was approached by a few girls, asking random question's about, where I had moved out of, if I had a girlfriend, and things of that nature. — I was introduced by these same girls, to some boy's at school. I was introduced to the popular kids in that school. And when I met this kid's, I felt at ease. I felt as though I fit right in. So I started bounding with these guys, until I was comfortable with calling them my friends.

Time flew by in school, and before I knew it I wasn't the "new kid" anymore; I was Lucky. A nickname that was given to me by these same friend's because of a tragic event we all experience and survived, especially me. — And just like that, what I was doing at my old town with my old friends; I was doin in this new town, with two handful of new friends. Just to a whole new level.

Somewhere down the line, about 1 or 2 year's later. I was introduced to drugs. Now I was expose to drugs at an earlier age, I just never consumed any of it. — But over here in this new town, with new friends, I started taking drugs starting with what is now legal in the State of California, Marijuana. — I can't exactly remember who pushed drug's into the scene. But it was something that became the norm for us. Once I started doin drug's, it as though we were doin it everywhere, even at school. — Mariguana lead to alcohol, alcohol lead to us experiencing harder drugs such as; cocaine, meth, and other substances. My grades started falling, my motivation towards school started dropping, and my attitude started changing. I was gettin distant towards my family, because I had developed a new family amongs my peers.

I became entwined in a web of alcohol and drugs, and my group of bad influences that the difference in me started to show at home and at school. In school, I started fighting with other kid's. And even fighting against my teachers. I was always gettin suspended from school. And when I would come back to school from a suspencion, that same day I would get suspended again for fighting. I was caught with drugs, weapons, and pictures of all sorts of thing's in my possesion. And I didn't care who caught, or seen any of it.

At home, when my parent's would come and get me from a suspension, they would yell at me, call me names, ask me why I go to school if all I do is get in trouble, and just verbally abuse me. But that was it. And once I seen that I wouldn't be gettin dissiplined at home physically, I started doin more in the streets and at school. — I got myself kicked out of numerous school districts, went to numerous continuation schools and it was always the samething. — Gangbanging, set trippin, drugs, alcohol, and girls. I was living a real fast life, at a real young age. I was living a destructive lifestyle that made me forget about my teenage years.

Goin back to my parents. Is not that my parents didn't care about me. Just that they didn't know how to approach the situations I was puttin them through. Out of six kids, one was the "black sheep" of the family, me. They couldn't focus their attention too much on one kid, when their were five others they had to look after. All my sisters were teenage mothers, they got themselves pregnet at a young age. So my parent's were put through a lot, not only with the behavior I was showing, but also with my siblings. Is just that my sisters or brother weren't out gangbanging, stealing, and committing crime's like I was. — But this is one of the reasons why I wasn't bein dissiplined at home. My parent's had a lot on their plates already to really focus on one misbehaving kid.

Ive always wanted my parent's attention. I never told them that, but I did. I wanted to feel their love more than it just bein material love. I felt that at times because of everything I was exposing them to, in a way the love they had for me was maybe diminishing a bit at a time. I felt that they didn't love me as much anymore because of my behavior. But these ideas and thoughts were just creating distance between my parents and I. Because my ideas were incorrect.

I dealt with these insecurities and low self esteem the only way I Knew how to. I hung out with my homies, smokin, doin drugs, and gangbangin. We would hurt our enemies, because thats exactly what they were, enemies. All the drugs I was consuming clouded my judgement. Because in all reality those guys weren't just enemies. They were human beings. With a family just like I, with a brother just like mines, and who Knows... probably even a father just like I.

Because of the ideology I had developed during this time. My beliefs made me look at these same indivituals as just a race, color, or enemy. My ideology labeled and stigmatized these same human beings as rivals of another gang, period. I wasn't concerned with representing this guys as humans, because I myself had lost my humanity. And these turn of events, were the consequences of my consumption of drugs, and participation in a gang.

Page 6

I'm an adult now. Serving a life sentence., because I didn't Know how to communicate to my parents, or open up to them and the counsulors that had reached out to me. as a troubled Kid. — I was afraid of bein myself. Because of my low self-esteem. I was afraid of facing rejection, so I played a variety of roles; a gangmember, drug addict, the Kool Kid, because that was my way of avoiding rejection. I wanted to stick with school, but afraid of bein judged or rejected by my peer's. So I didn't demonstrated any act towards schooling. And because of my lack of caurage. I struggled between; good or evil, nice or bad. — I lacked an identity of myself, and lacking this identity lead me to put a variety of different mask on. Which lead me into playin different roles as a teenager. I didn't Know who? I wanted to be, or become, I was lost.

As a teen I knew I wanted to do good in life., but I lacked the caurage to do so. And that lead me into a destructiv. lifestyle. People around me wanted to help, but I wouldn't want to pay that any attention. Because of my lifestyle. I had developed numerous drug addictions. I was at my lowest with my addictions. I even wittness my mothers suffering because of it. But I didn't care, because I was lost in the cycle of my addiction, with only one worry. When was my next high?

With drug's, I wouldn't spent my day's at home, rather in the streets, with my home boys. And for days I wouldn't come home. And whenever I did come home is was only to sleep, change clothes, and eat. And I was out-ant-about for the next few days. I was stealing cars, committing robbery's, and batteries, and I didn't realize that the only person I was hurting was myself. My parents suffered and went through a lot because of my addiction and behavior, and thats something I have to live with.

My parent's tried everything in their power, their very best effort to get me out of my destructive lifestyle cycle. They tried figuring out what I was goin through me, but couldn't because I was afraid to communicate with them. Not because I was afraid of what they would do to me, but because I was gettin tierd of hurting them. And also because I didn't want them to judge me for all the things I had done.

When I was goin through all this, I remember my parent's use to always say; that those same friends I was hanging out with, were the same ones that were goin to forget about me whenever I ended up in jail or prison. And I use to get upset. Because I thought my parent's were full of crap. That all they wanted to do was pull me away from my peers, so they would say anything in order for me to pull away. So I wouldn't pay attention to what they would say. But they tried lecturing me on life, they gave me everything, even when I was misbehaving. But none of it worked. Because I thought I had life all figured out. But how could I when I myself was only a kid. My behavior finally lead up to me committing a deviant act. I took a human life.

That was close to ten year's ago. I was 19th year's old, and only 21 years of age when I was given a sentence of 26 year's to life in prison. — Now... im fighting to get out of prison. And fighting for my life. And everysingle thing my parent's were telling me about, about my so-called "homies" came true. They forgot about me, some even did some dirty things behind my back. But none showed their support towards me, because none really cared. That was all part of the gangbanging lifestyle, but the only ones that really cared for me, and have been their for me and will be their for you... is the family.

I thank God for givin me the courage I needed to walk away from the gangs and drugs I was facing. Because bein in prison doesn't mean that those same drugs and gangs actually stop bein around. Because that cycle continues, if you allow it to continue. for yourself. — I thank God, because. once I've seen what this gangbanging lifestyle. is really about, and once I've seen who my true friends really were... and who was suffering from it all. Not my homeboys, or girlfriends, but my family were the only ones that were hurting from it all, and the only ones that have really been their for me. So after that, after seeing the facts, and takin the blindfold of my eyes... I walked away from it all, late... but man was it worth it.

Prison isn't pretty, it's an ugly enviornment with a lot of violence goin around it. More than what I was use to in the streets. And adapting to that same violence isn't humane, not to me anymore.. — You get use to it, use to seeing violence, just like anything else in life, you adapt. "But know right now", adapting to violence isn't something I wanted out of life. And it's something worth thinking about for yourself. Because you can always go deeper into that destructive pit we created for ourselves, but gettin out of it, is the real mission.

Everything that I believed in as a kid was only nothing but a fraud. I grew up in the streets, shooting at my enemies, hurting human beings, puttin in work", only to end up in prison, end up in the whole. Once their the same people who I was putting in work for, were the same ones who were lecturing me, to educate myself. Telling me to read books, to get back out into society. — Here I was hurting my family, my friends, girls I was with, ect. Only to find out that it was all for a cause with no meaning, no purpose. I realized it too late, with a life sentence on my back. Or if your one of the lucky ones with "Only" 15-20-25 years, but no life. Because that's a blessing in here, 20 year's, But what they don't tell you is that you come in to prison with 10 year's, only to end up with life later for still putting in work, for a no cause. You see I only heard what I wanted to hear, and the real advice that came from my family and real friends, was just ignored.

Thats why im reaching out to you, whoever you are. Please realize before it's too late., I Know its hard reaching out to your parent's or counclers. But speaking to them will only do you good. Don't let one bad decision be your downfall. Trust your parent's, the counclers, to whoever is their reaching out to you, because their the ones who care, care for you.

We only live once, don't waste it like many behind bars did. Enjoy live, and really educate yourself, because thats never too late to do. — Now im at a trying to change my values, my bad habits, my language, and even the way I look. Because all these new changes are who I really am. Now im educating myself, I've earned my G.E.D in prison, because I was too Kool for school and decided to drop out. — I'm in college now, goin after a degree, "in prison". With the help of many, even the state.

These are all the things I could of enjoyed and done out in society. But because I was afraid of bein myself, I let the enviornment I was in dictate my life and outcome. Don't let "fear" hold you back from fufilling your dreams. Anything is possible, dream big, and believe that you have the will to accomplish things for yourself, because you do.

Invest yourself with positive role models that want good for yourself. And that are not telling you to pick up a gun. Just trust yourself, because your really not alone. Your words, your actions carry a lot of weight. And your life is worth living out in society and not in a prison cell like me.

As a child, I couldn't identify my signs. My low self-esteem, and lack of identity. Neither could my parents. But I don't fault them for that anymore.. Because I Know that I was faced with internal and external factors that were pushing me towards a life of destruction And I shouldn't of allow those factors to define me.

I was never really alone, like I thought I was. My family was never absent towards me. I was bein influenced to believe that my family were the "homies" from the hood. And these are strong factors that work hard on Keeping you down and away from your loved ones. So if you see those signs, don't be like I was and fall for the bate. Be wiser, and stronger to choose the right path.

If I could do it all over againg. I would say no to drugs, no to Gangs, and no to bad influences. And I would go back and choose to become that nerd or geek I always had in me. — I've always wanted to help people. I wanted to become a paramedic. Funny how life turns out sometimes. I wanted to save lives, instead I took one. And thats something I'm dealing with, by approaching my flaws.

I'm involved in all sorts of self-help classes now. I'm taking courses that deal with; anger, alcohol, drugs, violence, gangs, empathy, and many more.. Because these were the flaws that I dealt with. — Years ago, I wouldn't of been able to identify what I was goin through. But because of effective programs like the ones I participate in, I'm able to pin point, and best of all... "learn" from the bad decisions I took. I Know we don't see these types of classes, and programs working for us in society. Because were not willing to give change, a chance. But if theirs something that I have learned from these same programs is, that, once you open yourself up and speak about whats on your mind and heart. Boy... do wonders happend. Because you will start to transform from that point on. —

Trust the process, is something I was told my first time I attendent these groups. And because I did, Im able to reflect and learn from my experiences. — So give it a try.

Let me tell you something, Your life matters to me. Because for all we know you could be someone that could change the world, society, or even your commonity. But you don't know that, because your not allowing yourself to find that out. — Be open to new possibilities, and I wish you best in life. And I hope that hearing from someone whos done it all in life, and im refering to the negative... and been through it all... can help you see the world from a different perspective. Grow and learn from your downfalls, and don't let it define you buddy.

"Your not alone, Remember that".

Sincery.

Inmate. Edgar Garcia #AI1860

Edgar Garcia

JARED PETROVICH

34 years old
First degree murder
Life

whats up groms! ☺ ha ha 4-21-17

Just wanted to send a shout out and let you know a bit of my story. I grew up skateboarding and surfing in Orange County. All was good. I got into pot, heavey drugs all the bad things just were so easy to do. Obviously I wish I didnt take the easy way. As I got locked up at a young age of 16 yr for possesion for sales of meth xx I did 14 months at YGC (youth Guidance Center) in Orange. I was in and out of Juvi went to Los Pinos. I was in 2A I took our baseball team to championships. Pinos! But ya I was in a downward spiral of addiction which led to "adult time" I stopped skateboarding and just lost myself in the meth. I was in and out of county Jail so many times not even caring or thinking long term. I was like "its only drug charges" Never thinking later on in life that cycle of addiction and getting locked up so much would lead to a life sentence for a murder! Sitting here writting you guys this I still cant believe it! Ive never been the violent type. To be honest I didnt even actually carry out the murder I was only a part of it (long story) but YA Im sitting in the hole for 5 1/2 years and now level 4 prisons for the last 10 plus years xx Due to enviornments I put myself in! So I just want to say "think" before you do some-thing. life is priceless we only get one shot at the title. And I know when I was young sitting in Juvi 2 unit waiting for court they would bring guys in to sit us down to try and help us. I never even listened to them so its hard for me to put myself in your shoes to relate just because I've been there where you are now only goes so far you have to actually care about yourself and your future. I understand I could talk till Im Blue in the face bottom line is its your life and you think you got your whole life ahead of you. And you do! I just want to drop a seed of thought to you and let it grow that life is PRICELESS... your priceless! And your AWESOME... if I ever get out of here Im going to build a safe place to kick it a skateboard park in the community for FREE, Just like the bad ass one at Vans in Orange. ☺

alright then Amazing people of our future please take just a sec. to think about what I've said. And remeber to enjoy life.

BTW! I was barely 21 yr. old when I got a life sentence, So Im sure you could see yourself there at that age, right?

Yours Truly,
Jared

JARED PETROVICH #AK-9285
D4-109 Lower
Po Box 5007
Calipatria, CA. 92233

p.s. Keep your nose in a book, and pray.

JOSEPH TAYLOR

31 years old
Carjacking, kidnapping, robbery
11 years to life

By: Joseph Taylor #AA-0629
D3-227 Low

4-22-17

To Whom It May Concern: Page. 1

I Want To Start This Off By Expressing My ~~Deep~~ Deepest Regretts For You Having To Be The One To Hear This. I Dont Wish Long Term Incarceration Upon Anyone. However Since This Is where We Are I Wanted To Talk To You The Way I Wish Somebody Would Have With Me When I First Came In.

Let Me Introduce Myself, I'm Joseph Taylor, 31 Yrs. Old. I'm Sentenced To 11 Yrs. To Life - 9 Yrs. For Cajacking, 2 Yrs. For A Weapon, $ Life With The Possibility For Kidnapping To Commit Robbery. - I've Been Down Since Dec. Of 2006 - Working On My 11th Year. After I Was Sentenced, I Convinced Myself, Basically Over Night, That I Wasn't Gonna Die Of Old Age In The Pen. I Was Already A Gang Member, Of "Orange County Skins". I Was Gonna Be The Meanest $ Most Ruthless Skinhead To Ever Enter The Cali. Penitentiary System. I Was 21 Yrs. Old When I Came In, Whenever Somebody Had To Be Beat Up Or Stabbed, I Volunteered Everytime. I Wanted To Be That Guy That Everybody Talked Highly Of $ Feared.

I Wanted All Of That Because Thats What Everybody Around Me Wanted. It's All Everybody Talked About, Well That $ Getting High. I Was Sentenced To Life $ Didn't See Myself Ever Getting. Because I Had No Body Who Cared Enough To Share Information $ Put Me Up On Game. But I'm Gonna Try To Break That Cycle, By Sharing What Knowledge I've Learned In The 10+ Years I Have In Here. It's Up To You, On What You Do With This Information.

I Know It's All Over Whelming. But You'll Adjust. The Quickest Way To Adjust Is To Sign Up For As Many Classes, & Groups & Programs As Possible. If They Have Sport Clubs, Football, Softball, Soccer, Basketball, Sign Up. If You Don't Have A High School Diploma Or GED. Sign Up For VEP. (Volentary Edeucation Program.) There's Usually A Couple ~~Moths~~ Months You'll Be On Waiting Lists. The Point Of Signing Up For Everything. Is To Keep Busy.

The Busier You Are, The More Time You Spend Going To Substance Abuse Classes, Or Anger Management. The Less Time You Have To Think About All The Negativity That Surrounds Us On A Daily Basis. It's Hard To Stay Out Of Trouble When Were Bored, By Sitting In Our Cell All Day. With Drugs Being Offered & Violence Being Displayed. And A Big Plus From That, Is When You Write Or Talk To Your Family & Loved Ones, And Tell Them About Your Day. Because They Will Ask. Trust Me. You Can Tell Them "Oh Mom, I Had My Alternative To Violence Class In The Morning. My A/A Class Tonite & My Basketball Team Won This Afternoon!". It Really Shows That You Are Trying To Stay Out Of Trouble. It Puts There Minds & Hearts At Ease.

Also, Another Positive Outcome Is You're Gonna Meet Some Cool Dudes That Are Trying To Do The Same Thing. So You'll Be Surrounded By Guys That Will Encourage You To Keep Going. To Not Give Up, To Encourage You To Sign Up For 1 More Class. To Share 1 More Time In

Group. Entice You To Read 1 More Book Or Just 1 More Chapter Out Of Your Bible.

Ok, Now I've Been Saving This For The End. So Listen Carefully. - No Matter What Anybody Tells You, Whether It's A C/O Trying To Get A Rise Out Of You. Or Another Inmate Trying To Break Your Stride Or Dampin Your Spirits. NO MATTER How Much Time You Have To Do. You Can Make It Out Of Here. Brother You Are Not Doomed, You Just Can't Waste Any Time Or Start Off By Getting Into Trouble. If I Would've Done Everything I Just Told You, I Would've Gone Home 7 Years Ago. I Didn't Have Anybody That Would Take The Time, To Take The Needle Out Of Their Arm & Put Me Up On The Things I Could Be Doing To Earn A Date To Go Home. And You Can't Expect, These C/o's Or Counslers To Point You In The Right Direction. We Are Just A Number On A Long List To Them. Now That You Know Their Are Things You Can Do To Get Out, All I Ask, Is That You Pass It Along. With A Message To The Next Guy To Pass It On.

Every Positive Or Negative Things You Do In Here Ends Up In Your C-File. Look, Yes Ur An Inmate In A Institution, That Doesn't Mean Ur A Failure & Ur Not Worth A Second Chance. You Are The Shot Caller Of Your Destiny. If You Want Out Of Here One Day, Then Fill That C-File With Positive Things, Diplomas, Certificates, Chronos Saying Ur Being A Model Inmate Or Outstanding Student

I Got A Late Start, And I'm Still Close To Getting A Parole Date. And I Have, Stabbings, Staff Asshaults, Participating In Riots, Fighting, Drug Use. But I Would Have Avoided All Those Things If I Had Somebody Write Me A Letter Like This One. So When This Opprotunity Was Presented To Me, I Leaped At It. To Hopefully Save You & Your Loved Ones Years Of Pain & Heartache. Remember You Aren't The Only 1 Doing Time. Your Family Is Being Held Prisoner Too. I Wish You The Best. & Pray For Success & A Reduced Sentence. I Hope You Found My Words Insightful. If You Doubt Them. Thats Fine, But Still Try, It Can't Hurt To Give It A Shot. You Atleast Owe It To Your Family To Try & Come Home As Fast As Possible. God Bless!

Respectfully,

JoJo

Joseph Taylor #AA-0629
D3-227 Low
P.O. Box 5007
Calipatria, Ca 92233

MANUEL FELIPE

25 years old
Murder
19 years to life

Who am I?

I am Manuel F. I have discovered who I really am. I am a human bieng who has made a bad decision in life and now paying the consequences of my action. I always valued my gang more rather than my family I thank GOD to helping me mature. It took Me 10 years for me to realize that the values of my gang didn't matter and did not have a future for me. I am happy to receive help threw the Self Help groups. Thanks to this programs I have been able to discover myself. I have learned to relieve my pain, anger and hatred threw pen and paper and not threw violence. Violence has got me no where and I have gain nothing. All I have gained is pain to my family and have hurt myself mentally and emotionally.

Choosing the path of crime which I became a gangmember got me to hurt my community. I was poisoning my own community with illegal drugs (heroin, Cocaine and meth). Stealing from innocent people who worked hard to earn what I stold from them. So this are few choices that I made in life and got me to prison.

All I am trying to say is lets stop creating victums, and lets stop hurting ourselves. It is never to late to change and mature. I hope that What I wrote here can inspire you to make the wright choices in life and do good. family comes first rather than gang. Love your community and lets be leaders and not followers. Let us be willing to receive the help offered and stop putting our self down. Thank You! May GOD BLESS You.

Respectfully
Manuel Felipe.

KEVIN PARADEZ

22 years old
Attempted murder
56 years to life

Who ever is reading this letter in C.Y.A or juvenillehall my name is Kevin Im 22 year old. Ive been locked up for seven years now. Honestly when I frist got locked up I was Scare, nervous, and confuse. I didn't Know what to expect, but I had that little braveness in me. That braveness is what help me get threw it. Im sure you guys have that braveness as well, right?

I was always fighting, talking back to the staff, and having that "I don't Care" attitude. I can say it was fun for me at times. Even though I had friends in here I felt lonley at times to, because I wasn't around people that I really, really Knew like my family, or my friends from the streets. I didn't show that side of me because I believed that was showing weakness.

Now that Im getting older Im realize ing that theres more in life then to just be in a prison cell. I said it was fun for me at one time, but it is not worth it, For me is not. Im missing out on seeing my family grow, missing out on freedom, and missing out on all the good thing I could of been doing with my life. So to all of you in C.Y.A or juvenillehall think before you act. You know right from wrong so do right and enjoy your life. Take care of yourself frist then others. Good Luck

ARNOLD BROWN

53 years old

"Where Would You Rather Be?"

A man recently said: "I am a product of [my] bad choices."

I am writing you because, like you, I am not where I want to be. Where would you rather be? I'd prefer being with my family and friends skateboarding, playing golf, or basketball. But here I sit in a cell with a lengthy prison term. How did I get where I am? Think about that, "How did [we] get to be where we are at?

I believe I am where I am because of some of the choices I have made in the past. Those decisions came together adding up to my present circumstances. Notwithstanding, if I want something different I need to do things differently (Note: If nothing changes, nothing changes).

I have come to realize that to get to where I want to be I need be wise in spending my "168". Each week I get "168" just like you! Seven days a week we get 168 hours to use as we wish. It's a gift. More than 60 hours we spend resting because the body and mind need and deserve it! After rest, we are left with about 100 hours. That comes out to 14 hours a day — give or take.

So, how are you spending your time? Be realistic by accounting for what your daily activities are and how much time is spent doing each (track your activities for a week; examples: exercise, reading, T.V., sleeping, keeping yourself clean and healty).

Once we have accomplished that goal we are in a better position to pursue some long and short term goals that will move us in the direction that will improve our lives and overall well-being. If we want to be with our families and friends then our daily choices need reflect that (Short term goals add up to long term goals).

Three years ago I set some goals that included writing you. My daily routine made such possible. As a Christian, I seek God's help and guidance in making the best choices I can make throughout the day. I sought His help in writing you. I know your saddness, frustration, anger, and fear.

ARNOLD BROWN 05/01/2017
Where Would You Rather Be?

I have written this to you because I believe you have the ability to make different choices than you have made. Look at it this way, make some different choices for a few days that will improve your well-being and outlook on life. You get to experience making better, healthier choices. I think you will like the results.

I believe you will always get the help you need at the right moment. We have God and a lot of people who care about us and want to help us. Together lets make better choices for ourselves. By doing so, we will be where we want to be with our families and friends. I'll be on a skateboard, playing golf, and basketball with those I love... what will you be doing?

One last thing:
'Success is found in our daily routine!'

See ya later! (¡Hasta Luego!)

Arnold Brown (ARNOLD BROWN)

RAYMOND ANTHONY LOPEZ

40 years old
Murder
100 years to life

This letter is to the ~~fou~~ thirteen year old me. I can rember how ackward I was back then, wondering about what my friends were thinking about my scuffed up shoe's or my faded clothes, or being embarresed that my parents were pisa & didnt speak one word of english. Hopeing that I was cool enough to hang out with. I didn't have one lick of sence back then, but I'm sure every body who did aint or has never once been in the sittuation I'm in now see that lil fat kid who was trying so hard back then is now a 40 year old man with a 100 years to life sentece with 19 years in the system on this term. Now I know hindsight is 20/20 beacuse I have lived in some sort of cell for more then half my life. Little did I know at thirteen that just 2 years later I would get picked up on a punk ass G.T.A & while in ~~juvinal hall~~ central juvinal hall the D.A would file on a residental shooting case & ask that I be tried as a adult. I rember while I was sitting in a chair in court that my feet couldnt even touch the ground, while the judge agreed with the D.A that you do the adult crime, you do the adult time & sending me on my way to do my my 90 day op. Shit everything was brand new to me then drugs, gang banging & hoodies thats all I thought about. So with this shine in my eyes I explained to my parents in spanish on my next court date that I had been found fit to be sent to prison. My mother cried the whole time, my dad told me be strong. "no llores", don't cry he said to me as I got sentenced to 7 yrs. I rember I was scared to look at the judge while he spoke so I just looked down at my scuffed up cortez while I swung my feet back and forth on the seat. Well I was just turning sixteen now so I didnt go directly to prison, I got to ~~ya~~ Y.A as a (M#) but I was going to be held there till my ~~18~~ eighteenth B-day, but fate wasnt on my side and another (M#) killed a female staff at the Y.A were I was at so state wide all (M#)'s were sent to adult instatutions. And I was sitting in a new cell in Wasco Reception Center. The older cats got at us like we were regulars a couple of soups, coffee, tabacco, deodorant & soap and I felt like a vet. And I was all in down for whatever wanting to once agein be cool enough to be accepted. So becuase of my lack of self worth, & for the most part not knowing any better I quickly found mysef in Ad-Seg & well by doing what I thought was my part for the cuase I soon picked up a SHU term, just 18 months but I was on my way to the big time "Corcoron SHU" pending transfer to Pelican Bay, the madness was that I was acting like I had nothing to lose but nobody cared enough to let me know what consaquences were waiting at the end of this road. Well out of nothing but luck did I make it out of "Corcorn" bewteen the cut throat sureño politics & the cops seting up cock fights I maxed out my 7 yrs and didn't catch any new cases & ~~par~~ paroled. But I had just turned 21 and wasn't in anyway ready for the streets, my head was so full of bullshit I got out thinking about trying to stay out as long as possible

BUT KNOWING I WAS COMING BACK, WELL REALITY SLAPPED ME RIGHT OUT THE GATE YOU NEED TO EAT SO YOU GOT TO WORK AND NOBODY WANTED TO GIVE A FELON A JOB. NEEDLESS TO SAY LIVING IN PRISON IS EASY COMPARRED TO TRYING TO MAKE IT OUT IN THE FREE WORLD. NOTHIN IS FOR FREE SO I GOT FRUSTRATED WITH THE SHIT END OF THE STICK I WAS GETTING TRYING TO DO RIGHT & AT MY ~~to~~ LOWEST DECIEDED TO GO BACK TO THE HOOD OF COURSE I WAS EMBRASED AS A PRODIGAL SON RETURNED. DRUGS, SEX & GANGBANGING BUT WITH A COLDER DETERMANATION I HAD SEEN HOW SIMPLE VIOLENCE, BLOODSHED, DEATH WAS IN THE SYSTEM & I BECAME THAT ANIMAL THAT I NEEDED TO BE IN THE SHU JUST FOR MY MIND TO STAY SANE IN THERE, BUT NOW ON THE STREETS WITH WHAT I THOUGHT WERE NO CONSAQUENCES. I MEAN AFTER ALL THERE WASN'T NO GUN TOWER ON THE STREETS & THAT SHIT DIDNT STOP ME IN THE SYSTEM SO FUCK IT! WELL I TOOK A LIFE WITH THAT FRAME ~~ON~~ OF MIND. STOLED SOMBODY'S WHOLE FUTURE ANY POSSIBILITYS ~~THE~~ HE MIGHT OF HAD OUT OF IGNORANCE, NO APOLOGYS OR ANY ATTEMPT AT AMENDS THAT I MIGHT DO CAN EVER BRING THAT LIFE BACK, BUT JUSTICE ~~HAS~~ WAS SERVED AND THE SYSTEM BROKE ME OFF A 100 TO LIFE SENTENCE SO IN A IRONIC WAY I TOOK A LIFE AND GAVE MINE AWAY. SO THIRTEEN YEAR OLD ME MAKE SOME CHOICES THAT WILL MAKE YOU WISE BEYOND YOUR YEARS. BECUASE LIFE ISN'T ALWAYS GARENTEED AND ANYTHING YOU DO IN THIS LIFE TIME SHOULD ECHO THREW ETERNITY. YOU ONLY GOT ONE SHOT AT THIS SO MAKE EVERY DISCION COUNT AND LOOK TOWARDS YOUR FUTURE WITH HOPE IN YOUR EYES!

RAYMOND
LOPEZ J-40838

JOEL BAPTISTE

41 years old
Murder
Life without parole

Joel Baptiste

Life Without Parole,I came to prison in the late 90s-early 200 era of zero opportunities for any lifer to be released,much less a kid with a (LWOP) sentence. I was twenty years old when I was involved in a murder. I was not the primary,meaning that I was not the person who actually committed the act of murder. Because of that I carried a huge chip on my shoulder,I failed to see my part in the chaos of that night. I felt that I had been railroaded by the justice system,coupled with my ignorance in youth and the violent world that I had just stepped into,I was a kid **WITHOUT HOPE!** I had lost an amazing girl,my family and ultimately my status as a human being.

I started to get indoctrinated into the prison culture. I started to see my friends getting butcherd literally for minor infractions or drug debts. The last straw came while witnessing a close home boy get his throat sliced with a box cutter and almost bleeding to death behind a door. The powers that be cast his lot among the losers that day in the political arena that would soon become my life. I decided that day that I would make my own fate and never be a victim,pure survival mode kicked in.

Prison was very violent in those days. I am from Orange County,I belonged to a group that was notoriously criminal,and political (PEN#1) Public Enemy Number One or (PDS) Pen#1 Death Squad. A skin Head gang which exhibited all the misguided pomp and thirst for the best that us Orange County boys carried on our sleeve. Violence and politics were the currency of our lives in prison and I started networking,utilizing every chance I could to climb the political ladder. This meant raising my hand all the time to go on missions inflicting violence on other inmates. It was not long before I started planning these missions. My whole goal was to exert maximum violence and have my shooters get away. In reality the greed of climbing the ladder and little political victories fueled the misplaced youthful ego. Eventually I started getting major directives,lists of people who were important that needed to go! Sometimes my friends would appear on these lists and if they were in my prison I would try to help them but in the end the monster dictates **"YOU OR THEM"**.

Years go by and you carry these deeds with you. No matter how callous you believe yourself to be it is only the hierarchy of needs that really pushes you through the moments. Humanity will catch up with you,late at night, those acts will come back to you and you will contemplate them.

Eventually after touring the state of California's level four yards,recreating that insane no brain cycle,I landed in New Folsom where I was validated for association with The Aryan Brotherhood. I had done many SHU terms prior to this but this was the first time that I was given a a sentence in prison that matched my controlling case. I was given an indeterminate SHU term and sent to what was then headquarters for all gang activity (PELICAN BAY SHU).

I thought "Ok I made it ,I can kick back now and do what I want,regain some autonomy". **Far from reality!** tHIS NEW Life in the SHU was for keeps. I remember getting up to answer a call on the tier of my ASU wing where I was waiting to go to my SHU housing. I thought I would be fishing in some much needed supplies that me and my celly needed. When I retrieved the transporter under the door it contained a piece with a note that said remove your celly/take his wind. I understood this meant to remove him from life if possible. As the Guards and medical staff were pulling us out of the cell I was being dragged through my friends blood and pepper spray when I heard him gasp at me "**I THOUGHT YOU WERE MY FRIEND**". That was the last straw for me even though I didn't yet end the chaos,what had I become? We were just eating breakfast together and sharing.

I bring you to this next point not to criticize or boast but to present the facts that others won't to you,to give you the truth.

As I sat in the Pelican Bay SHU program year after year 1,2,3,4,5,6,7 they just kept ticking away. Life outside was moving on,family members had died and many new ones had been borne. I was not there for any of that life or apart of any life outside those corridors. I believe that in all of the years and gnarly hunger strikes,violent episodes and times of dull silence that the Sun actually hit my skin directly about twenty or so times,and that was just a glance as it crept in from the thirty foot walls and small square above the SHU yard.

All the old men were just that (OLD MEN) Pale as if on deaths door and these were the wizards behind the proverbial curtain that we were sacrificing our lives and families for. I had seen the ugly truth. When you first get to prison you are hit with a skewed re-education process where your cultural history and identity are manipulated to fit the paradigm of the gang and it's survival. It is a serious calculated system organized to **extort** your usefulness and then you are cast aside or you move up. If you want to be a gangster my friend,just save yourself the trip and re read these truths that I put my life in jeopardy to share with you.

My heart prays that you listen to this next part. YOU DON"T NEED TO TAKE THESE ROADS ANYMORE! that die is broken! There is a new path,society has changed along with CDCR and the legislation.

Trip, that kid I was grew up,I am now engaging in every opportunity that the state of California will offer! I am in a FACE TO FACE College program with Imperial Valley College,I have a 4.0 (GPA) the highest you can obtain and state recognition with The Presidents Honor Roll. By the time that you read this I will have my Degree! I want to tell you that **Now more than ever HOPE is alive**,**YOU CAN change**,**I DID.** I promise you that you have a success story inside of you. I was a failure at everything but evil,but I made one good decision,then another,and another. It kept getting better,better than any vice.

You are my little brothers,I failed at my primary family and my own little brother,I can't be with him and I didn't get to help him grow up in truth. But because of **HOPE** I refuse to fail you! I want you to make a decision to succeed and be a real leader. Flip the stigma. I promise you I still represent Orange County but now my community needs me,it doesn't loath me! Until we dive inside ourself and solve the problems or seek help our community says that we belong here and here we willstay,I get it now!

You now have what I didn't have at the begining,society and communities are reaching out to you. Grab that hand home boy,I promise you that you won't regret it **EVER.**

Joel Baptiste
@ Calipatria State Prison 2018
STUDENT/Inmate second.

Just so you know,there is no avenue at the moment for me to go home. this is all about freedom inside,almost all of you have the chance to go home though if you listen to me.

AUTHORS

GLOSSARY

AD-SEG	Administrative Segregation (for inmates on the way to the SHU)
The Aryan Brotherhood	Extremely violent white gang in control of all white gang activity
Black Gorilla Family	Political group active in publishing newsletters regarding unconstitutional prison practices
Bloods	Political black street gang
Calipatria State Prison	Maximum security prison located in Calipatria, California, twelve miles from the border of Mexico. The prison, built in 1992, was designed for 2,000 people, but currently houses over 4,000 inmates.
CDC	California Department of Corrections
C-File	Central File (a central file containing all personal records)
Crips	A black street gang with very old political ties inside and outside of prisons
DOJ	Department of Justice
Fishing	When an inmate uses string to get goods from another cell
GTA	Grand Theft Auto
HDSP	High Desert State Prison
IGI	Institutional Gang Investigations Unit
Level 4	Second highest prison security level
LWOP	Life without parole

M#	Identification number for minors
Mexican Mafia	Powerful Mexican organized crime entity
Nazi Low Riders	White gang that originated in Y.A.
Norteno	Mexican street gang from Northern California under direction of the Nuestra Familias
Nuestra Family	Equivalent of the Mexican Mafia, but from the north and with different political views
PC	Protective Custody (for individuals who no longer want to be involved in gang activity)
Pisa	A Mexican national who doesn't speak English, and is likely an illegal alien
SB260	Senate bill that allows for minors who were charged with life to be considered for parole
SHU	Security Housing Unit (a prison within the prison)
Skinheads	Racial separatists identified by the FBI as terrorists
Surenos	Southern Mexican street gang under control of the Mexican Mafia
YA	Youth Authority (where juveniles are housed)

www.ingramcontent.com/pod-product-compliance
Lightning Source LLC
Chambersburg PA
CBHW041134100726
47911CB00003B/125
* 9 7 8 0 6 9 2 1 0 6 1 2 9 *